GROSS STUFF IN YOUR HOUSE

BY PAM ROSENBERG

ILLUSTRATED BY BEATRIZ HELENA RAMOS

ABOUT THE AUTHOR:

Pam Rosenberg lives in Illinois with a husband, two kids, two cats, a hermit crab, a few bugs, and lots of bacteria and other tiny things she doesn't like to think about.

ABOUT THE ILLUSTRATOR:

Beatriz Helena Ramos is an artist from Venezuela who lives and plays in NYC. She works from her animation studio, Dancing Diablo, where she directs animated spots. Beatriz has illustrated a dozen books and she particularly loves gross stories.

The Child's World

Published by The Child's World®
1980 Lookout Drive • Mankato, MN 56003-1705
800-599-READ • www.childsworld.com

Photos: CSIRO, CC BY 3.0, via Wikimedia Commons: 5; Donenko Oleksii/Shutterstock.com: 19; IrinaK/Shutterstock.com: 8; OlgaReukova/Shutterstock.com: 12; Suzanne Tucker/Shutterstock.com: cover

ISBN 9781503850231 (Reinforced Library Binding)
ISBN 9781503850712 (Portable Document Format)
ISBN 9781503851474 (Online Multi-user eBook)
LCCN: 2021930091

Printed in the United States of America

TABLE OF CONTENTS

YECCH!

THERE ARE ALL KINDS OF GROSS THINGS OUT IN THE WORLD.

Strange animals, germs, weird plants, dirt, pollution—all kinds of yucky stuff. Maybe we should stay home where it's nice and clean and cozy! But don't look too closely—what you find at home might be scarier than the stuff outside. Let's take a tour of the gross place you call Home!

SNEEZE AND SNOT PRODUCERS

What lives in your mattress, eats dead skin cells, and is too small to see without a microscope? **Dust mites!** There could be millions of them living in your bed right now. The nice, warm, moist **environment** of your cozy bed is like a fancy hotel for dust mites. Your body sheds lots of dead skin cells every day. Many of the dead cells end up in your bed, **providing a feast for the dust mites** living there.

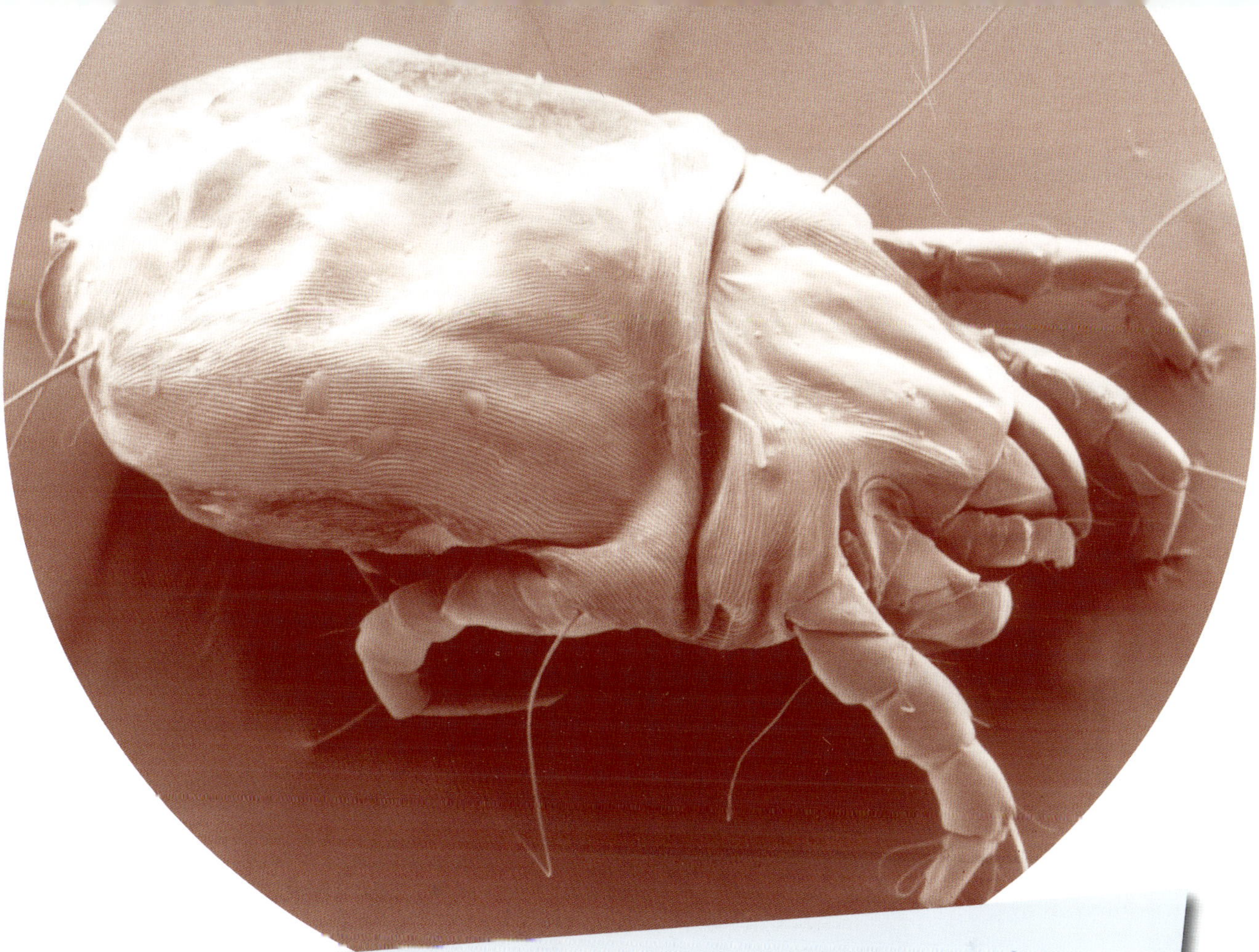

Dust mites are related to spiders and ticks. Most people can live with dust mites and not give them another thought. They don't bite and because they are so small, you never see them. But people who are allergic to them definitely know they are around. When the dust mites grow, they shed their skin. That **old skin, along with dust mite poop,** is what makes some people's noses run and their eyes water. So try not to think about the dust mite poop in your mattress when you close your eyes to go to sleep tonight!

Do you have a dog or cat? If you do, you might think that there isn't anything gross about your cute, furry friend. But some people sneeze whenever they are around Fido or Fluffy. Lots of people think it is cat and dog hair that causes an allergic reaction in some people, but it's not. Dander is what causes the watery eyes, runny nose, and sneezing of animal allergies. What's dander? **Dander is the tiny flakes of dead skin from furry or feathered animals.** That plus their dried up saliva is what usually causes people with allergies to be miserable around pets.

Here's another fact about **pet dander**—it's very sticky. **It sticks to shoes, clothes, carpets, and just about anything else it comes in contact with.** So, even if you decide to get rid of your pet to get rid of your allergies, you might still have a reaction when you go into your house. Some experts say it can take months of regular, thorough cleaning to get the dander down to a level that won't cause symptoms anymore.

COCKROACHES AND OTHER CREEPY VISITORS

Having visitors come to your house is usually fun. Friends come over to play and family members come for parties. Those are good visitors. But there are some other visitors that most of us prefer not to find in our homes. At the top of that list for many people are **cockroaches**. These brown, 1/2-inch to 1-inch (1.25-cm to 2.5-cm) long bugs have long **antennae** and move quickly. They usually come out at night when it is dark, and they will eat anything. If they get in your house, you will have a hard time persuading them to leave. Your warm, cozy house is like a good hotel with a great restaurant. Besides food, **they'll eat soap, glue on stamps, paper, and just about anything else they can find.**

Lots of people think that cockroaches are dirty, but they are really very clean. They spend hours every day cleaning themselves. So what's the problem with having them in your house? Well, besides the fact that they are creepy, **they leave behind lots of teeny, tiny piles of poop.** And that poop is a problem for people with allergies and **asthma**—it can make them cough and **wheeze**. Another problem is that they can reproduce very quickly. One female German cockroach can produce about 500,000 babies in just one year!

Another buggy visitor you don't want in your house is the **carpenter ant.** These 1/4-inch to 1/2-inch (6-mm to 1.25-cm) long ants like to build their nests in wood. If you give them enough time, **they will hollow out the wooden beams that hold your house together.** You can probably guess what happens if they do that—better hope the house falls down when you aren't home!

Night, night, sleep tight, **don't let the bedbugs bite!** These little wingless bloodsuckers like to live in furniture, especially furniture that people sleep on. When they are hungry, they look for an unsuspecting human or other animal and **drink some of their victim's blood.** If you wake up in the morning with some itchy red bites, you may have been a meal for a bedbug or two.

Have you ever seen something with lots of legs crawling up a wall in your house? If you have, you've probably seen a **centipede**. The house centipede has fifteen pairs of legs and can move very quickly when disturbed. But before you grab something to smash the life out of that gross-looking bug, think about this: Centipedes are **carnivores**. **Some of their favorite foods are cockroaches, bedbugs, and other pesty visitors**. Still want to kill that leggy creature?

GERMS!

There is no avoiding the tiny **microorganisms** that share our world with us. **They are everywhere.** Most of them are harmless, but some of them cause diseases like colds, flu, and strep throat, to name just a few. Bacteria are one kind of microorganism. These single-celled germs reproduce by dividing in two. They do this about every 20 minutes. So **one teeny-tiny bacteria cell can become millions of cells in just 24 hours!**

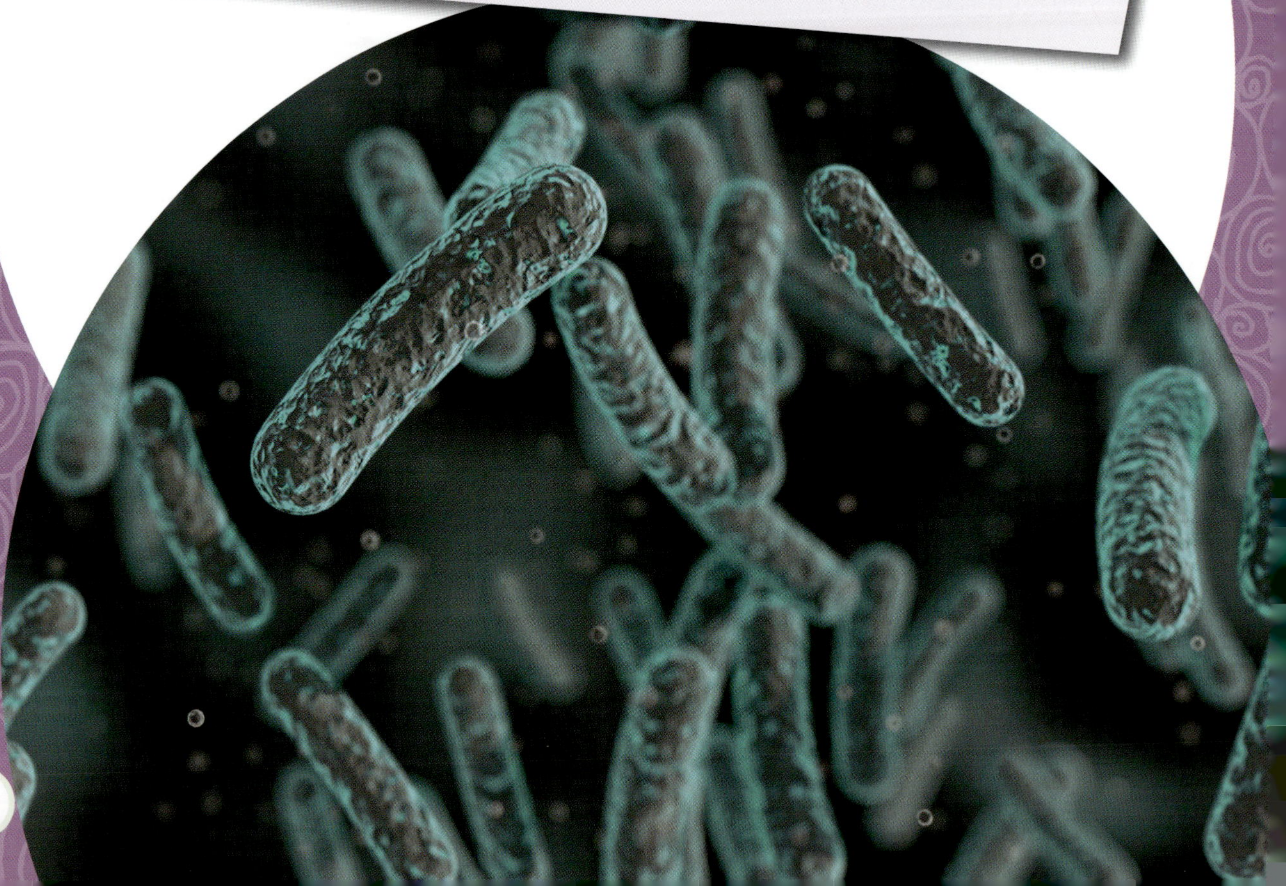

Which room in your house do you think is the germiest? If you said bathroom, you're wrong! Your kitchen is the germiest room in your house and **the sponges and dishcloths in your kitchen sink are probably the most germ-filled items** in your kitchen. So next time your mom says that it's your turn to wash the dishes, you can try getting out of it by telling her that you don't want to go near all those germs. But don't be surprised if she tells you to wet the sponge or dishcloth and put it in the microwave oven for two minutes. Yep, a little microwave cooking will zap those germs and you'll be up to your elbows in dishes and soapy water before you know it!

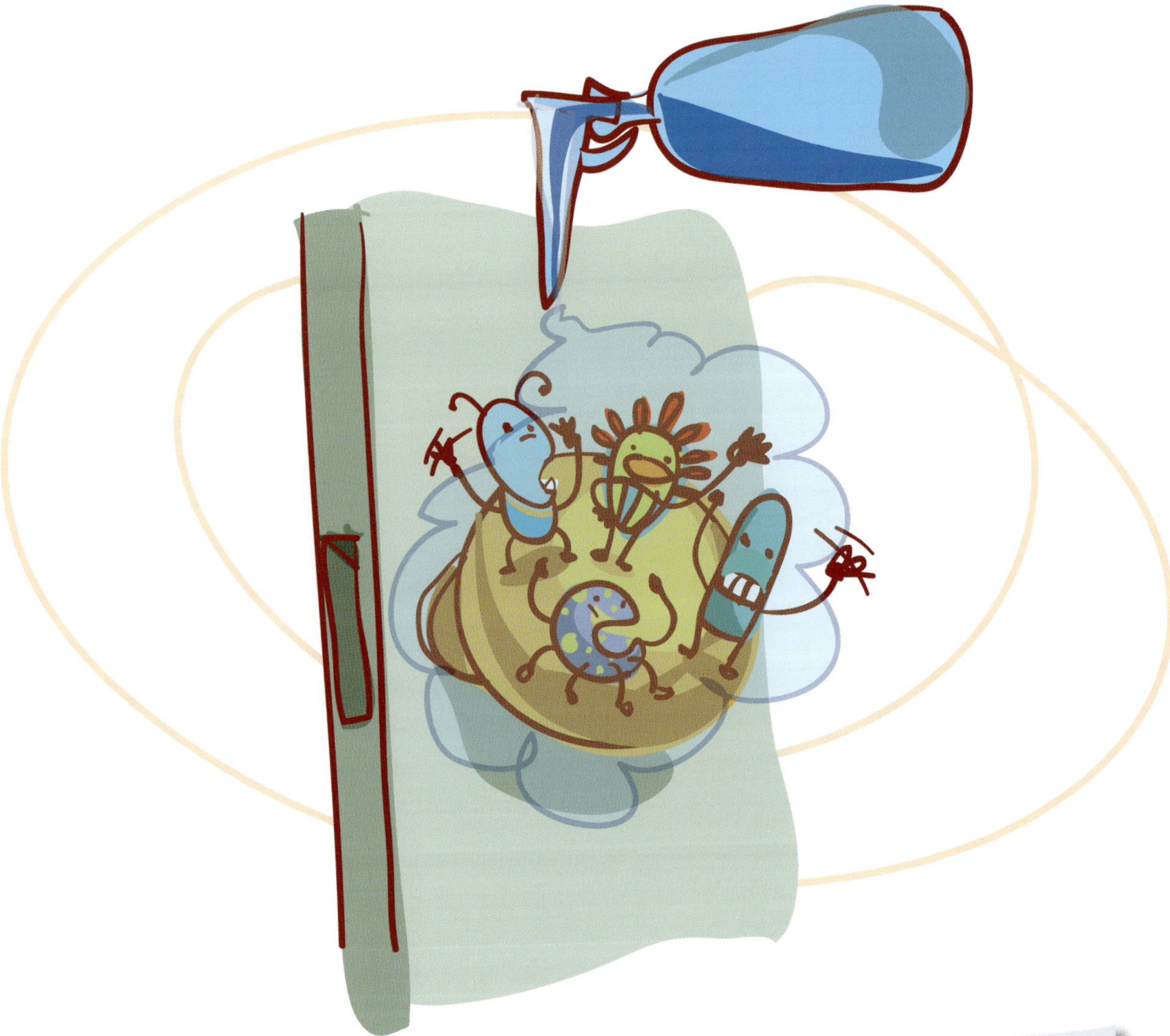

What other surfaces are likely to spread germs from one person to another in your house? **Kitchen and bathroom sink drains, sink faucets, and doorknobs are all germy.** Cleaning them often with a household cleaner that kills bacteria and viruses will help keep the germ population down and help keep everyone healthy.

PUTRID POOP

Okay. Most of us don't have poop laying around our houses spreading nasty germs. Well, except for maybe the tiny, microscopic kind left behind by the little bugs that share our houses with us. But if you stop to think about it, you may realize that there is a small poop machine in many households—a baby! Do you have a baby brother or sister? Then you have poopy diapers in your house—at least you do until someone takes out the trash. **Not washing your hands after changing a poopy diaper is one of the quickest ways to spread the germs that cause diarrhea.** And if everyone in your house ends up with that problem, there's going to be a lot more poop in your house!

Do you ever wonder where all that poop goes after you flush your toilet? In many places it ends up in a system of underground pipes called **sewers** that run beneath the streets of your city. The toilet in your house is connected to pipes in your house that lead to this system of sewer pipes. Those pipes lead to a **sewage** treatment plant. Bacteria that like to munch on poop and other waste and chemicals are added to the sewage. Eventually all the gunk is separated into liquids and solids. Then the liquids get dumped into the nearest body of water (try not to think about that the next time you go swimming in the local lake!). All of the solid goo ends up in landfills or gets burned in really big **furnaces**.

In some places without a fancy sewer system, your poop and other waste don't make such a long journey. Instead, houses have a **septic tank**—a big concrete container buried in the yard. All of the waste heads off to the big container. The **liquid waste drips out of the container and into the ground.** The solid stuff ends up at the bottom of the tank. Every couple of years, someone has to pump the solid waste out of the tank to make room for more solid waste. Does pumping out septic tanks sound like a job you'd like to do when you grow up?

MOLDY MATTERS

Mold is a member of the **fungus** family. Like sneakers, they come in all different colors. They can be blue, pink, orange, or green. Some of the less colorful varieties are white and black. **The biggest living thing in the world is a mold.** It is a fungus known as honey mushroom and there is one specimen in Malheur National Forest in Oregon that is 3.5 miles (5.6 kilometers) across. It is bigger than 1,600 football fields! Scientists who study these kinds of things think that this giant fungus is at least 2,400 years old. If you go there you won't see one giant mushroom. Most of the organism is underground.

If you don't want to travel all the way to Oregon to see some fungus, don't worry. If you haven't cleaned out your **refrigerator** in a while, all you have to do is look inside. **There is probably some kind of mold growing on food in there.** How does the mold grow on your food? There are millions of microscopic mold **spores** (kind of like mold seeds but you can't see them) floating around in the air. Try not to think about them the next time you take a breath. When you leave food on a table or counter, some spores are likely to land on it. Under the right conditions, the spores start to grow and send tiny threads into the food to digest and use the food's nutrients.

So, if you find food with a tiny spot of mold on it, **can you still eat it?** That depends. **Most of the time the answer is no,** especially if the food is soft and has a lot of moisture in it. That's because the mold you see is just a small part of the mold. There is probably more mold under the surface where you can't see it (remember that giant mold in Oregon?). But food safety experts say there are some foods you can eat if you **cut the moldy spot off**—things such as hard cheeses, firm vegetables (such as cabbage and carrots), and hard salami. Just cut off the moldy spot or, in the case of the hard salami, scrub it off the surface. Salami and cheese sandwich, anyone?

There are actually some kinds of cheese that are made with mold. On purpose! If you've ever eaten **blue cheese or Gorgonzola, you've eaten mold.** That white surface on Brie? Mold. **Yum!**

So, here's the bottom line. Some people make a special trip to the store to buy moldy cheese. Others keep cockroaches for pets. **What's gross to one person might be a special treat to another.** It all depends on how you look at it!

GLOSSARY

antennae (an-TEN-ee) Antennae are the feelers on the head of an insect. Cockroaches have long antennae.

asthma (AZ-muh) Someone who has asthma has a condition that sometimes makes it hard to breathe. Cockroach droppings can trigger an asthma attack in some people.

carnivores (KAR-nuh-vorz) Carnivores are animals that eat meat. Centipedes are carnivores that eat other insects.

environment (en-VYE-ruhn-muhnt) An environment is the surroundings that influence how a person or animal lives. A bed is a good environment for a bedbug.

fungus (FUN-guhss) A fungus is a living thing that produces spores for reproduction. Mold is fungus.

furnaces (FUR-niss-ez) Furnaces are large enclosed structures in which fuel is heated. Some solid wastes are burned in large furnaces.

microorganisms (mye-kroh-OR-guh-niz-umz) A microorganism is a living thing that is too small to be seen without a microscope. Bacteria are microorganisms.

sewage (SOO-ij) Sewage is the liquid and solid waste that is carried away in drains and sewer pipes. Sewage flows down drains and through sewers and ends up in sewage treatment plants or in septic tanks.

sewers (SOO-uhr) Sewers are underground pipes that carry away liquid and solid waste. Sewers carry wastewater away from homes.

spores (SPORZ) Spores are tiny reproductive cells produced by fungi and plants. The air we breathe is filled with millions of mold spores.

wheeze (WEEZ) If you wheeze, a whistling sound is made in your chest when you breathe. Some people with asthma wheeze when they are exposed to cockroach droppings.

FOR MORE INFORMATION

Gravel, Elise. *The Cockroach.* Toronto, ON: Tundra Books, 2021.

Harris, Nancy. *In This Kitchen.* Chicago, IL: Raintree, 2010.

LaPlante, Walter. *I'm Allergic to Dust.* New York, NY: Gareth Stevens Publishing, 2019.

McDonald, Megan. *Stink It Up!: A Guide to the Gross, the Bad, and the Smelly.* Somerville, MA: Candlewick Press, 2013.

National Geographic Kids. *Weird But True! Gross.* Washington, DC: National Geographic, 2016.

Visit our website to learn more about gross stuff in your house:
childsworld.com/links

Note to Parents, Teachers, and Librarians: We routinely verify our weblinks to make sure they are safe, active sites—so encourage your readers to check them out!

INDEX